A Frantic Assembly
and Theatre Royal Plymouth production

THE BELIEVERS

by Bryony Lavery

The Believers was first performed on 21 February 2014
at The Drum, Theatre Royal Plymouth

In association with Curve theatre, Leicester

The Believers contains strong language

Supported using public funding by
**ARTS COUNCIL
ENGLAND**

LOTTERY FUNDED

Cast

in alphabetical order

Christopher Colquhoun	**Joff**
Penny Layden	**Maud**
Richard Mylan	**Ollie**
Eileen Walsh	**Marianne**

Creative Team

Bryony Lavery	**Writer**
Scott Graham	**Direction and Choreography**
Jon Bausor	**Design**
Eddie Kay	**Associate Movement Direction**
Andy Purves	**Lighting Design**
Carolyn Downing	**Sound Design**
Sarah Hughes	**Casting Director**
Cathal Cleary	**Associate Director** (Tour)
Michaela Kennen	**Voice Coach**

Production Team

Hugh Borthwick, David Harraway, Nick Soper	**Production Managers**
Joni Carter	**Company Stage Manager**
Hayley Stafford	**Technical Stage Manager**
Zoe Spurr	**Lighting Supervisor**
Hamish Bamford	**Sound Supervisor**
Dina Hall	**Costume Supervisor**
Matt Hoyle	**Drum Technician**
Cheryl Hill	**Wardrobe Mistress**

For The Drum, Theatre Royal Plymouth

Simon Stokes	**Artistic Director**
David Prescott	**Artistic Associate**
Louise Schumann	**Artistic Co-ordinator**
Anne-Marie Clark	**PR Manager**
Laura Evans	**Marketing Manager**
Fran King	**Education Producer**

Set, props and costumes by Theatre Royal Plymouth

For Frantic Assembly

Despina Tsatsas	**Producer**
Inga Hirst	**Learn and Train Manager**
Fiona Gregory	**General Manager**
Donna Marie Howard	**Office and Digital Administrator**
Jess Williams, Jonnie Riordan	**Learn Associates**
Joe Public Marketing Ltd	**Marketing**
The Corner Shop PR	**Press**
Helen Maybanks	**Production and Rehearsal Photographer**
Matthew Haysom, Matthew Hodges	**Graphic Design**

Thanks

Frantic Assembly would like to thank the following people and places for their support of *The Believers*:

Theatre Royal Plymouth.

Charles Aitken, Charlotte Alexander, Mark Arends, Matt Barker, Suzanne Bell, Ed Bennett, Rebecca Brower, Sofie Burgoyne, Julie Crofts, Noma Dumezweni, Sharon Duncan Brewster, Vicky Featherstone, Delphine Gaborit, Mariah Gale, Iain Gillie, High Performance Rigging, Steven Hoggett, John Ellerman Foundation, Roger Luckhurst, Lisa Maguire, Victoria Meagre, Caroline Meer, David Miller, Kate O'Flynn, Henry Pettigrew, David Prescott, Justin Salinger, Louise Schumann, Simon Stokes, The Jerwood Space, Andrew Upton, Fabi Waisbort, Richard Winsor, Tom Wright.

Produced in association with Curve theatre, Leicester.

Cast Biographies

Christopher Colquhoun
Joff

Christopher trained at RADA, since which he has had an extensive career both on stage and screen. Most recently on stage, he was seen as 'Mister' in The Menier Chocolate Factory's hit show *The Color Purple,* for which he was nominated for Best Featured Actor in a Musical at the Broadway World Awards.

Other theatre credits include *A Midsummer Night's Dream* (Regent's Park Theatre), *Britannicus* (Wilton's Music Hall), *Happy Now?* (Hull Truck Theatre), *Five Guys Named Moe* (Theatre Royal Stratford East and the Edinburgh International Festival), *Troilus and Cressida* (Shakespeare's Globe Theatre), *The Thief of Baghdad* (Royal Opera House), *Three Sisters* (Royal Exchange Manchester), *Saint Joan* (National Theatre), *Comedy of Errors* (Royal Shakespeare Company), *Simply Heavenly* (Trafalgar Studios), *Ain't Misbehavin'* (Derby Playhouse), *Blues in the Night* (Birmingham Rep), *Snake in the Fridge*, *The Way of the World* (Royal Exchange, Manchester), *Angels in America* (Crucible Theatre, Sheffield), *The Slow Drag* (Whitehall Theatre), *Romeo and Juliet* (US tour), *Five Guys Named Moe* (National tour), *Moby Dick*, *King Lear*, *The Tempest*, *The Merchant of Venice* (Royal Shakespeare Company), *Woza Albert*, *Gates of Paradise* (Royal Shakespeare Company Fringe).

Christopher was nominated for Best Actor in a Supporting Role at the Manchester Evening News Theatre Awards for his portrayal of Banquo in *Macbeth*, at the Royal Exchange Theatre, under Matthew Dunster's direction.

Despite his significant theatre credits, Chris is probably still most recognisable as Dr Simon Kaminski from *Casualty*. Most recently, he was seen in *Law and Order* for ITV.

Other television credits include *The Crash* (BBC3), *Missing* (ABC Studios), *Coronation Stree*t (ITV Granada), *Wire in the Blood* (Carnival Films), *Belonging* (BBC), *North Square* (YTV), *Silent Witness* (BBC), *London Bridge* (Carlton), *Band of Gold* (Thames), *Shakespeare Shorts* (BBC) and *The Bill* (Talkback Thames).

Penny Layden
Maud

Theatre credits include *Edward II, Table, Timon of Athens* (all National Theatre), *Nora* (Belgrade Theatre, Coventry), *66 Books* (Bush Theatre), *Incoming* (Hightide), *Lidless* (Trafalgar Studios, Edinburgh, Hightide), *Vernon God Little, The Art of Random Whistling* (both Young Vic), *The Bacchae, Mary Barton, Electra, Mayhem* (all Manchester Royal Exchange), *Dancing at Lughnasa* (Birmingham Rep), *The Spanish Tragedy* (Arcola), *Romeo and Juliet, Helen, Hamlet, The Antipodes* (all Shakespeare's Globe), *Cinderella* (Old Vic), *Comfort Me With Apples* (Hampstead Theatre/Tour), *Assassins* (Sheffield Crucible), *Popcorn, Season's Greetings* (both Liverpool Playhouse), *The Laramie Project* (Sound Theatre, West End), *A Passage To India, The Magic Toyshop, Jane Eyre* (all Shared Experience), *The Tempest, Measure for Measure, Roberto Zucco* (all

RSC), *The Winter's Tale, Ghosts* (Lyric Hammersmith/Tour), *What I Did In The Holidays* (Drill Hall/Tour), various seasons at the New Victoria, Stoke.

Television credits include *Call The Midwife, Prisoner's Wives, Land Girls, Sirens, South Riding, Silent Witness, Poppy Shakespeare, Doctors, Bad Mother's Handbook, Waterloo Road, No Angels, The Bill, Murphy's Law, Outlaws, Fat Friends, M.I.T, Casualty.*

Film credits include *Broken, The Libertine*.

Radio credits include *Crime and Punishment, Second Chance, Uganda, Return Ticket*.

Richard Mylan
Ollie

Previous work for Frantic Assembly includes *Peepshow*.

Other theatre credits include *Baggage* (Arts Theatre*), How I Helped End Communism* (The Lowry Studio*), Crazy Gary's Mobile Disco* (Paines Plough*), Badfinger* (Donmar Warehouse*), Starlight Express, The Shoot.*

Television credits include *Waterloo Road* (BBC/Shed Prods), *Casualty* (BBC), *Doctors* (BBC), *Grown Ups* (BBC3), *My Family* (BBC), *Where The Heart Is* (ITV), *Belonging* (BBC Wales), *No Angels Everything I Know About Men, Coupling V* (Hartswood/BBC), *Bad Girls* (ITV), *Wild West I & II* (BBC), *Score* (BBC), *A & E* (Grenada), *Belonging I & II* (BBC), *Welcome To Orty Fou* (Carlton), *The Bill* (Thames), *Border Café* (Hartswood), *Dirty Work* (Pearson), *Couples* (LWT), *Tech Heads* (Celador), *Silent Witness* (BBC1), *The Demon Headmaster* (BBC), *Beer Goggles*.

Film credits include *City Rats Upside of Anger, Love, Peace and Pancake, Check out Girl, Snarl Up, Dead on Time, The Wisdom of Crocodiles, Speak Like A Child.*

Radio credits include *A Taste of Honey* (BBC Radio Wales).

Eileen Walsh
Marianne

Previous work for Frantic Assembly includes *Tiny Dynamite.*

Other theatre credits include *Liolà* (National Theatre), *Conversations, Whistle in the Dark, Famine, Hamlet, Request Programme, Medea, Macbeth, The Gigli Concert, Terminus, The Playboy of the Western World, Saved, Mary Stuart, The Merchant of Venice, Portia Coughlan, Crave, Ariel, The Drowned World, Splendour, Troilus and Cressida, Boomtwon, Disco Pigs, Phaedra's Love.*

Television credits include *Pure Mule.*

Film credits include *Gold, Snap, The Ballad of Kid Kanturk, Triage, The Maid of Farce, Eden, 33X Around the Sun, Nicholas Nickleby, Magdalene Sisters, When Brendan Met Trudy, Miss Julie, Janie Beard, The Last Bus Home, Spaghetti Show, The Van.*

Creative Team Biographies

Bryony Lavery
Writer

Bryony Lavery's plays include *Her Aching Heart* (Pink Paper Play Of The Year 1992), *Last Easter* and *A Wedding Story* (2000). Her play *Frozen*, commissioned by Birmingham Rep, won the TMA Best Play Award, the Eileen Anderson Central Television Award, was produced on Broadway where it was nominated for four Tony awards. Her previous Frantic Assembly collaborations include *Stockholm,* which won the Wolff-Whiting award for Best Play of 2008, and *Beautiful Burnout. Beautiful Burnout* premiered at the Edinburgh Festival Fringe 2010 and won a Fringe First Award, before touring the UK extensively in a co-production with National Theatre Scotland. It also toured to America, Australia and New Zealand before returning for a further UK tour in 2012.

Other work includes the heart-rending *Last Easter*, produced at The Door, Birmingham Rep, *Kursk* with Sound and Fury at The Young Vic UK and Sydney Opera House, *A Christmas Carol* at Birmingham Rep, an adaptation of *The £1000000 bank note* for BBC Radio 4, *Thursday* for ETT/Brink (Adelaide), *Cesario* for National Theatre, *Dirt* for Studio Theatre, Washington DC, an adaptation of Armistead Maupin's *Tales of the City/More Tales of the City* for Radio 4, *A Doll's House* at Manchester Royal Exchange and *Thursday* ETT/Brink Theatre at Adelaide and Canberra Festivals.

Bryony is a Bruntwood Playwright Associate at Manchester Royal Exchange, an Associate Artist at Birmingham Rep and an honorary Doctor of Arts at De Montfort University and a Fellow of The Royal Society of Literature.

Scott Graham
Director and Choreographer

Scott Graham is Artistic Director and co-founder of Frantic Assembly. He is the co-choreographer of *The Curious Incident of the Dog in the Night-Time* for which he received an Olivier Award nomination for Best Theatre Choreographer. For Frantic, he has co-directed *Little Dogs* (with National Theatre Wales), *Lovesong, Beautiful Burnout* (with National Theatre of Scotland, Fringe First Award), *Othello* (TMA award – Best Direction), *Stockholm, pool (no water), Dirty Wonderland, Rabbit, Peepshow* and *Underworld.* Director/performer credits include *Hymns, Tiny Dynamite, On Blindness, Heavenly, Sell Out, Zero, Flesh, Klub* and *Look Back in Anger.* Scott Graham's other directing credits include: *Home* (National Theatre of Scotland) and *Ker-ching* (Sixth Sense). He has also provided choreography and movement direction for *Praxis Makes Perfect* for National Theatre Wales; *The Canticles* at Brighton Festival/Aldeburgh Music; *Port, Hothouse* and *Market Boy* at the National Theatre; *Dr Dee* for Manchester International Festival/ ENO; *Beauty and the Beast* and *Cinderella* at the Unicorn; *Frankenstein* for the Royal & Derngate; *The May Queen* at Liverpool Everyman; *Villette* at Stephen Joseph Theatre; *Dazzling Medusa* and *A Bear Called Paddington* for Polka; and *Stuart Little* on tour. With Steven Hoggett and Bryony Lavery, he created *It Snows,* a

National Theatre Connections play. With Steven Hoggett, he has written *The Frantic Assembly Book of Devising Theatre* (2nd edn., Routledge).

Jon Bausor
Designer

Jon studied Music at Oxford University and the Royal Academy of Music in London before training on the Motley Theatre Design Course. He designed the Opening Ceremony of the 2012 Paralympic Games in London.

Theatre design includes: *Ghost Stories* (West End, London/ Toronto/ Moscow); *KURSK* (Young Vic/ Sydney Opera House); *Lord of the Flies, To Kill A Mockingbird* (Regents Park Open Air Theatre); *Lionboy* (Theatre de Complicite); *Romeo and Juliet* (Abbey Theatre, Dublin), *I am Yusuf* (Shebbahurr, Palestine/ Young Vic), *Water* (Filter Theatre) and *Terminus* (Abbey Theatre, Dublin/ Melbourne/ New York/ Boston), *The Birthday Party* (Lyric, Hammersmith).

As an associate artist of the Royal Shakespeare Company he has designed numerous productions including *Hamlet, King Lear, The Winter's Tale* and the entire 2012 season entitled *What Country Friends is this?*

Dance design includes: *Hansel and Gretel, Ghosts, Pleasure's Progress* (Royal Opera House); *Scribblings, Castaways* (Ballet Rambert); *Blood Wedding* (Finnish National Ballet), *HOWL* (Bern Ballet, Switzerland/ Joyce Theatre, New York), *Snow White in Black* (Phoenix Dance Theatre); In Media Res (Nederlands Dans Theater) and *Firebird* (Norweigan National Ballet)

Opera design includes *The Knot Garden* (Theatre an der Wien); *Queen of Spades* (Festival Theatre, Edinburgh); *The Lighthouse* (Teatro Poliziano, Montepulciano); *The Human Comedy* (Young Vic, London) and *The Soldier's Tale* (Old Vic, London/ Baghdad).

Eddie Kay
Associate Movement Director

Previous work for Frantic Assembly includes *Hymns, Dirty Wonderland, Othello, Beautiful Burnout*.

Movement Director Theatre credits include *The blue boy, Have I no mouth* (Brokentalkers), *Smiler* (National Theatre of Scotland), *Crash Test Human* (freshness), *The Radicalisation of Bradley Manning* (National Theatre Wales), *dead born grow* (Frantic Assembly/National Youth Theatre Wales), *The Pass* (Royal Court).

Associate Movement Director credits include *Once*.

Dance and theatre credits include *Cost of Living, To Be Straight With You* (DV8), *Knots, As You Are, Faun* (CoisCéim), *Bird with Boy, The Falling Song* (Junk Ensemble); *Track* (Brokentalkers).

Opera credits include *Dr Dee* (Rufus Norris and Damon Albarn).

Film credits include *Cost of living* (DV8 Films), *Round 10* (Channel4) *Motion Sickness* (Junk Ensemble).

Andy Purves
Lighting Designer

Lighting designer working primarily in visual and movement-based theatre, circus and educational projects.

Andy trained in sound and lighting engineering at the University of Derby and has an MA in lighting design and theatre-making from Central School of Speech and Drama, where he also tutors in lighting.

Previous work for Frantic Assembly includes *Stockholm, Beautiful Burnout, Lovesong, Little Dogs.*

Lighting designs include projects made with: Frantic Assembly; The Sherman, Cardiff; The Young Vic; New Perspectives; Inspector Sands; The Gate; Spymonkey; The Barbican, London; Sydney Theatre Company; Caroline Horton; Northampton Royal; Stan Won't Dance; Tamasha; Brighton Festival; Cartoon de Salvo; National Theatre Wales and National Theatre of Scotland.

He designs regularly for Circus Space, has toured extensively with Propeller and worked on La Clique and La Soirée at The Roundhouse and in the West End.

Carolyn Downing
Sound Designer

Previous work for Frantic Assembly includes *Beautiful Burnout* (with National Theatre of Scotland), *Little Dogs* (with National Theatre Wales) and *Lovesong*.

Sound design credits include *Chimerica, Blood Wedding* (Almeida); *Protest Song, Double Feature* (National Theatre); *Handbagged* (Tricycle); *How The Whale Became* (ROH); *American Lulu* (The Opera Group); *King John, The Gods Weep, The Winter's Tale, Pericles, Days of Significance* (RSC), *The Pass, Circle Mirror Transformation, The Low Road,The Witness, Our Private Life* (Royal Court); Fanny Och Alexander (Malmo Stadsteater); *Amerika, Krieg der Bilder* (Staatstheater Mainz, Germany), *After Dido* (ENO at Young Vic), *Lower Ninth, Dimetos, Absurdia* (Donmar Warehouse), *All My Sons* (Broadway), *Tre Kroner-Gustav III* (Dramaten, Stockholm), *Angels in America* (Headlong Theatre), *To Kill A Mockingbird, The Country Wife, A Whistle in the Dark, Moonshed* (Royal Exchange Theatre), *3rd Ring Out* (Metis Arts), *Gambling* (Soho Theatre), *Lulu, The Kreutzer Sonata, Vanya, State of Emergency, The Internationalist* (Gate Theatre), Blackta, *After Miss Julie* (Young Vic), *Belongings* (Hampstead Theatre), *After Miss Julie, Othello* (Salisbury Playhouse); *Andersen's English, Flight Path* (Out of Joint); *The Water Engine* (Theatre 503).

Sarah Hughes
Casting Director

Sarah Hughes has been Alan Ayckbourn's casting director since 1991, casting world premieres of his plays at the Stephen Joseph Theatre Scarborough, in the

West End, at the National Theatre and on Broadway, as well as many other productions at the Stephen Joseph Theatre. Since 2000 she has also freelanced for the BBC, where series include *Jonathon Creek, Grass, Love Soup, Parents of the Band, 2 Pints, Pulling,* John Sullivan's *Rock & Chips, The Old Guys, Freedom* and *The Great Outdoors*. Freelance theatre work includes plays for the West Yorkshire Playhouse, Birmingham Rep, and Theatre Royal Northampton, and *The Believers* is her fifth project for Frantic Assembly. In 2011/2012 she was one of four Senior Cast Co-ordinators for the London 2012 Olympic and Paralympic opening and closing ceremonies, leading on the Paralympic Opening. In 2013, she cast the BBC1 6-part series *Slings and Arrows*, and recent projects include world premieres of John Godber's *Muddy Cows* and Alan Ayckbourn's *Arrivals and Departments*, revivals of *Time of my Life* and *Sugar Daddies* at the ACT Theatre in Seattle, plus *Laughton, The Schoolmistress* and *Beauty and the Beast*, for the SJT.

The Believers 2014

The Drum, Theatre Royal Plymouth
21 February – 8 March
www.theatreroyal.com

Warwick Arts Centre, Coventry
11 –15 March
www.warwickartscentre.co.uk

Curve, Leicester
18 – 29 March
www.curveonline.co.uk

Tricycle Theatre, London
22 April – 24 May
www.tricycle.co.uk

Schools resources are available for this production.

For further information about the online resource pack,
videos, workshops and more visit
www.franticassembly.co.uk

franticassembly

'The vibrant and visceral Frantic Assembly'   *Independent*

Frantic Assembly creates thrilling, energetic and unforgettable theatre. The company attracts new and young audiences with work that reflects contemporary culture. Vivid and dynamic, Frantic Assembly's unique physical style combines movement, design, music and text.

Frantic Assembly is led by Artistic Director Scott Graham. Scott formed the company with Steven Hoggett and Vicki Middleton in 1994 and continues to collaborate with many of today's most inspiring artists. Having toured extensively throughout the UK, Frantic Assembly has built an enviable reputation as one of the most exciting companies in the country. The company has also performed, created and collaborated in 30 different countries across the world.

In addition to its productions Frantic Assembly operates an extensive Learn & Train programme introducing 6,000 participants a year to the company's process of creating theatre, in a wide variety of settings. Frantic Assembly also delivers Ignition, an innovative vocational training project for young men, particularly targeting those with little previous experience of the arts.

Artistic Director	**Scott Graham**
Executive Producer	**Despina Tsatsas**
Learn and Train Manager	**Inga Hirst**
General Manager	**Fiona Gregory**
Office and Digital Administrator	**Donna Marie Howard**
Learn and Train Assistant	**Laura Rolinson**
Creative Associate	**Neil Bettles**

Learn and Train Practitioners: Sofie Burgoyne, Zachariah Fletcher, Delphine Gaborit, Tomos James, Eddie Kay, Steve Kirkham, Imogen Knight, Vicki Manderson, Simon Pittman, Jonnie Riordan, Krista Vuori and Jess Williams

BBC Performing Arts Fellow: Dritan Kastrati

Trustees: Sian Alexander (Chair), Mark Ball, Ben Chamberlain, Julie Crofts, Alan Finch, Sally Noonan

Email: **admin@franticassembly.co.uk**
Website: **www.franticassembly.co.uk**
Phone: **020 7841 3115**

Productions

Little Dogs	Scott Graham and Steven Hoggett	2012
Lovesong	Abi Morgan	2011
Beautiful Burnout	Bryony Lavery	2010/12
Stockholm (Australia)	Bryony Lavery	2010
Othello	William Shakespeare	2008
Stockholm	Bryony Lavery	2007
pool (no water)	Mark Ravenhill	2006
Dirty Wonderland	Michael Wynne	2005
On Blindness	Glyn Cannon	2004
Rabbit	Brendan Cowell	2003
Peepshow	Isabel Wright	2002
Heavenly	Scott Graham, Steven Hoggett and Liam Steel	2002
Tiny Dynamite	Abi Morgan	2001
Underworld	Nicola McCartney	2000
Hymns	Chris O'Connell	1999
Sell Out	Michael Wynne	1998
Zero	Devised by the Company	1997
Flesh	Spencer Hazel	1996
Klub	Spencer Hazel	1995
Look Back in Anger	John Osborne	1994

Productions co-produced by Frantic Assembly and Theatre Royal Plymouth to date include: *The Believers*, *Lovesong*, *Othello*, *Stockholm*, *pool (no water)*, *Rabbit*, *Peepshow*

Frantic Assembly is a charity registered in England and Wales 1113716

Like us on Facebook **facebook.com/franticassembly**

Follow us on Twitter **@franticassembly**

Visit our online forum **franticassembly.co.uk/forum**

To find out how you can support the work of Frantic Assembly visit **franticassembly.co.uk/support**

 THEATRE
ROYAL
PLYMOUTH

*'Geography [is] still everything in British theatre. If the Drum
Plymouth was in London it would be feted as it deserves'*
Lyn Gardner, *The Guardian*

The Theatre Royal Plymouth is the largest and best attended
regional producing theatre in the UK and the leading promoter of
theatre in the South West.

There are three distinctive performance spaces: The Lyric,
The Drum and a small workshop/development space, The Lab.

The Theatre Royal Plymouth serves the South West with a wide
range of theatre including classic and contemporary drama, musical
productions and the presentation of national opera, ballet and
dance companies.

It also specialises in the production of new plays and has built
a national reputation for the quality of its innovative work,
particularly in The Drum.

Theatre Royal Plymouth hosts unrivalled set, costume, prop-making
and rehearsal facilities at its architecturally award-winning
production and learning centre. The site also accommodates the
majority of the Theatre's Creative Learning programme which aims
to creatively engage with a broad spectrum of young people and
communities in Plymouth and beyond.

Recent Theatre Royal Plymouth productions include:

Grand Guignol and *Horse Piss for Blood*, both by Carl Grose

Chekhov in Hell by Dan Rebellato

The Astronaut's Chair by Rona Munro

Forever House by Glenn Waldron

Solid Air by Doug Lucie

The Theatre Royal Plymouth also collaborates with
selected artists in the UK and beyond. Longstanding partners include:

Frantic Assembly (*The Believers, Lovesong, Stockholm, Othello, pool (no water), Rabbit, Peepshow*)

Told by an Idiot (*My Perfect Mind, The Horse You Rode In On, The Fahrenheit Twins*)

Ontroerend Goed (*Sirens, Fight Night, A History of Everything, Audience, Teenage Riot*)

Paines Plough (*Love, Love, Love* by Mike Bartlett, *Long Time Dead* by Rona Munro, *Mercury Fur* by Philip Ridley, *The Straits* by Gregory Burke)

Royal Court, London (*The Empire* by DC Moore, *Stoning Mary* by Debbie Tucker Green, *The Girlfriend Experience* by Alecky Blythe)

'Plymouth's Drum is a real powerhouse of innovative theatre and collaboration'
The Guardian

Chairman	**Sir Michael Lickiss**
Chief Executive	**Adrian Vinken OBE**
Artistic Director	**Simon Stokes**
Commercial Director	**Paul James**
Production & Technical Director	**David Miller**
Creative Learning Director	**Victoria Allen**
Marketing & Sales Director	**Marianne Locatori**
Theatre Manager	**Jack Mellor**

Registered Charity Number: 284545
www.theatreroyal.com

Director's Note

Of course, Bryony Lavery was the obvious choice to collaborate with on a production about the deeply personal and subconscious world of our belief systems. Nobody does subterranean complexity like Bryony!

I have collaborated many times with Bryony and each time her mind and poetry exhilarate me. *The Believers* fizzes with an energy that is so much more than the words on the page. Over the next few weeks we will be exploring this play's dark layers, finding it's aching heart and bringing it to life. I think it is a beautiful play about need and just what we are capable of when that need takes over. It is about the dangers of a closed mind and the potential of the impressionable mind.

I am also so excited about working with Eddie Kay. Eddie has performed in many Frantic Assembly shows and his creativity and tenacity have been invaluable. This time he is not performing but is by my side. I am buzzing with the potential of what we can achieve together with this remarkable cast. This is my first collaboration with designer Jon Bausor and already his brilliant set is opening up this world in a way that is sending me home full of ideas and itching to come back in the next day. Eddie, Jon, lighting designer Andy Purves and sound designer Carolyn Downing presents something of a dream team for me.

An integral part of that team is also Simon Stokes and his Theatre Royal Plymouth colleagues. Simon has been a massive supporter and mentor to me. It would not be possible for Frantic Assembly to make the work it does without Simon and Theatre Royal Plymouth. Similarly it would not be possible to tour without the bold programming of the Curve, Leicester, the Tricycle Theatre, London, and Warwick Arts Centre. Their theatres give a home to our work at a time when there is so much pressure on touring venues and we are looking forward to bringing *The Believers* to their venues.

SCOTT GRAHAM

The Believers

Bryony Lavery's plays include *Last Easter* (Manhattan Classic Company), *A Wedding Story* (Sphinx) and *Frozen* (TMA Best Play 2001, Eileen Anderson Best Play 2001) which opened at Birmingham Rep, moved to the National Theatre, and was then produced on Broadway where it was nominated for four Tony awards. Recent work includes *Kursk* (Sound and Fury), *The Wicked Lady* (New Vic, Stoke-on-Trent), *Stockholm* (Frantic Assembly/Sydney Theatre Company), which received the Wolff-Whiting Best Play 2008, and, with Jason Carr, *A Christmas Carol* (Birmingham Rep/West Yorkshire Playhouse). *Beautiful Burnout* premiered at the Pleasance Forth, Edinburgh, in 2010 (Frantic Assembly/National Theatre of Scotland). She is an honorary Doctor of Arts at De Montfort University and a Fellow of the Royal Society of Literature.

also by Bryony Lavery from Faber

PLAYS ONE
(*A Wedding Story, Frozen, Illyria, More Light*)

MORE LIGHT
SMOKE
LAST EASTER
BEAUTIFUL BURNOUT

BRYONY LAVERY

The Believers

ff

FABER & FABER

First published in 2014
by Faber and Faber Limited
74–77 Great Russell Street, London WC1B 3DA

Typeset by Country Setting, Kingsdown, Kent CT14 8ES
Printed in England by CPI Group (UK) Ltd, Croydon, CR0 4YY

All rights reserved

Copyright © Bryony Lavery, 2014

The right of Bryony Lavery to be identified as author
of this work has been asserted in accordance with Section 77
of the Copyright, Designs and Patents Act 1988

*This book is sold subject to the condition that it shall not,
by way of trade or otherwise, be lent, resold, hired out
or otherwise circulated without the publisher's prior consent
in any form of binding or cover other than that in which
it is published and without a similar condition including
this condition being imposed on the subsequent purchaser*

All rights whatsoever in this work, amateur or professional,
are strictly reserved. Applications for permission for any use
whatsoever, including performance rights, must be made
in advance, prior to any such proposed use, to United Agents,
12–26 Lexington Street, London W1F 0LE. No performance
may be given unless a licence has first been obtained

A CIP record for this book is available
from the British Library

978-0-571-31575-8

FSC
www.fsc.org
MIX
Paper from
responsible sources
FSC® C101712

2 4 6 8 10 9 7 5 3 1

Characters

Two sets of parents
Marianne
Joff

Ollie
Maud

The presence of two children
Grace
Joyous

Location
Now, somewhere . . .

Thanks to

Scott Graham for his magical ideas
and trusting me with them . . .

all the enormously bendy and brilliant
actor/dancers in the workshops and production . . .

Suzanne Bell for her great notes . . .

and Frantic Assembly for asking me
to work with them again!

THE BELIEVERS

BELIEF

The psychological state in which an individual
holds a proposition to be true . . .

Wikipedia

The odd line lengths
weird   spacing
and plethora of exclamation marks
and question marks in the text
are the author's attempt to convey
the frenetic nature of these characters
in their situation.

ONE

Now.
 It is outside.
 A woman, Maud, approaches . . .
 Imperceptibly, she is counting her steps . . .
 She stops by a wall.
 Her hand touches the wall.
 Her counting has reached . . .

Maud
 One hundred and twenty-three.

 (*She turns.*)

 (*She looks towards a building one, two, three paces in the direction she came from . . .*)

 One hundred and twenty-three!

 You   *Fool!*

TWO

Now.
 Inside.
 Somewhere near.
 A couple, Marianne and Joff . . .

Marianne
 I can't *bear* this.

 Let's start with what we *know.*

 What was *definite.*

Joff

Okay.

(*And they think deeply until . . .*)

Marianne

The weather was spectacularly *strange*.

Joff

Yes.

Marianne

Weird. Thunder lightning and *the rain*!!!
At that time of year . . .

Joff

Which *They* described as an 'Act of God'.

Marianne

Act of *God*.
Was it?

Joff

Well   you . . .

Marianne

No!

Not *that*!

(*Her hands may be at her ears as some horrible doubt
stalks them until . . .*)

Joff

Let's just concentrate on what we *know*

Marianne

We were *all* inside their house.

Joff

Yes

Marianne

Both sets of parents were round the dining table.

They
Only ever left to go into the kitchen to fetch things.
Didn't go *near* the bedroom.

Joff
That's what they *said*

Marianne
Swore to.
On their Holy Fucking Book!

We   us two   were at the table . . . until you

Joff
Went for a pee

Marianne
Said you went for a pee. *Said*.

Joff
I *did*.
Upstairs. Their bathroom.
I went in, *peed*, flushed, washed my hands, came
    down again.

Marianne
Said you did that. *Said*.
And you didn't do *anything* else . . .?

Joff
This again?

No!!!!

Why won't you believe me???

Marianne
You *know* why!

Why the upstairs bathroom?
Why not that little one downstairs by the front door?

Joff

I don't *know* why!
I was in a strange fucking house?
Perhaps I forgot there was a downstairs loo?
Perhaps I just wanted to see their upstairs? Snoop a bit?
Perhaps they *directed* me upstairs . . .

(*They try to remember.*)

Marianne

There's too many fucking '*Perhaps*' with you, Joff!!!

Joff

The *Perhapses* are all in *your* head!
There's *nothing* about me you don't *know*.
Jeezus!

(*Silence.*
 She doesn't believe him.)

You however . . .
Different story.
Am I right?
Am   I   Right?

Marianne

Don't start with *that* again.
We *went* through that.
You *have* to believe me.
It wasn't *important*.

Wasn't.
Isn't.

It *isn't.*
Honestly.

(*He doesn't believe her.*)

Please.

(*He doesn't believe her.*)

Fuck you, Joff!
FUCK YOU!

Okay. What we *know.*
Stick to that.

(*What do they know?*)

The girls were playing in *her* bedroom
This is what we know.

Joff

We heard them laughing

Marianne

Her. We heard *her* laughing.
That *Thing.*
We didn't hear them *both* laughing.

Joff

Didn't we think they were both –

Marianne

You thought you heard them *both* laughing.

Joff

I remarked on that!
I said!
At the table!

(*It's new and hopeful.*)

Marianne

Yes . . . *Yes!!!!*

(*Both their minds go back to this possible moment.
For a bit . . . it is possible that . . .
But then . . .
No.*)

But when we went through it for the police
You couldn't be *sure.*

Joff

No.
I couldn't be sure.

(*Beat.*)

I just *wanted* her to be laughing.

THREE

Maud is in the same place as Scene One, but smoking or
something . . .
　Ollie arrives.
　Hesitates when he sees Maud there, looking in that
direction.
　Eventually . . .

Maud

Well

Ollie

All peaceful.
She was with the nice one. The middle-aged . . . with
　the –

Maud (*slight mime of*)

Dyed 'just for *a lark*!' red bit . . .

(*Ollie's head slightly nods.*)

(*Nasty impersonation of . . .*) 'Claire'

'Call me Claire.'

Ollie (*it should be comical*)

They were doing something with 'puppets'.

Maud

Puppets?

(She shakes her head, normally, in disbelief.
    Then she shakes her head viciously to dislodge
belief.)

Ollie
    Don't do that.

(She stops shaking her head.
    She smokes or something.)

FOUR

Joff and Marianne there, same place.
    Watching.

Joff
    I wonder   now   if the girl had any   *assistance.*

Marianne
    He   went into the kitchen *three* times.

Joff
    Fucking '*Ollie*'!

Marianne
    A serving spoon for the *peanut* sauce

    Another bottle of 'this awesome Rioja'

    Just getting the 'It's actually *antique* silver' sugar bowl

Joff
    She never left the table.

Marianne
    Yes!
    She went into the kitchen for *something*

Joff
    What?

Marianne

Said she went into the kitchen for something.
Said.

Joff

She came back with fucking *nothing* in her hands!

Marianne

She seemed drunk then.
All *giggly*.
How much had she drunk . . .?
I *thought* when she came back she might be drunk.
Drunk as a *skunk*.

Joff

The key word here is *seemed*.
Seemed drunk as a skunk.

Marianne

Well . . . she *was* all *over* the place.
Later on.

Joff

That wasn't the drinking.
That was the *smoking*.

Marianne

Oh yes that was the fucking 'smoking'
We were so *stupid*!

Joff

We can't remember how much *he* was drinking.

Marianne

A lot.

Joff

A lot.
Yes.
A *lot* was drunk.
Wasn't it?

Marianne
Shut up

Joff
And
Was he 'smoking'?

Marianne
We'd had more than we're used to.
I know that.
I'll *never* forgive myself for that

Joff
It wouldn't have made any diff/erence

Marianne
Shut up SHUT UP!

Joff
That's what the police said.

Marianne
What the –

(*Contemptuous apostrophe-fingers accompaniment.*)

'Family liaison officer' said.
That's just what they *say*.
That's   they think that's *Comfort*.
Patting down the Parents.

Don't believe *that*.
That's just *lying*. *Institutional* lying.

Why do you do that?

Joff
What?
What?

Marianne
Always believe everything anybody tells you?

Joff

I don't!

Marianne

You *do*!
For a bit.
For a while.
Get all excited and *leapy* and 'It's possible Marianne
    it's possible you just need to open your mind and
    emoshuns to the wonderful possibilities, Marianne!!'

You buy into *lies*. You *do*!

Joff

Well . . . who bought into the *biggest* lie, Marianne?
Whose *emoshuns* got out of hand???
Who *really* opened her mind to the wonderful
    possibilities?
Who?

(*Silence.*)

Sorry.

(*Silence until . . .*)

Marianne . . .

Marianne

If *we* hadn't been drinking and trying that stupid
    smoking
We'd be *clearer* about whether *he* helped his kid *his kid!*
To do what she what she *did* to our daughter!!!!

FIVE

The same place outdoors . . .

Ollie

Maud.

Baby . . .
Let's go inside it's

Maud

One hundred and twenty-three.
Yards. *Paces. Steps.*Whatever.
To *their* house.
From *our* house.

Ollie

You didn't you should/n't go past . . .

Maud

Seventy-five from their house to the *hippies'* cottage!

Ollie

We're supposed to keep away from . . .

Maud

Eighty-three to the Lewis-Seymours.
With the grey door.
Sorry.
'Not *grey*!'
'Elephant's breath'

It had to be *us*
It had to be *you.*
There were *two* houses nearer
Who could have *should* have invited them in
But
It was *us*
It was *you*

Ollie

Please.

Maud

Fool!
Fools!

Ollie

It's cold, Maud.
Come inside.
Please.

(*But she doesn't . . .*)

SIX

Now
And they lay the table as . . .

Marianne

Joyous!
Their fucking golden fucking perfect fucking brilliant
sweet-hearted radiantly golden girl!

(*Quoting Ollie.*) 'Maud named her after one of her
orgasms!'
Smug fucking . . .

Joff

What we don't know is how it happened.
Was it intentional?
Was it just a mistake?

Marianne

'Just' a mistake

You're unbelievable!

Joff

I'm just *trying to understand!!!*

(*A new thought.*) Wait.

Marianne

What?

Joff

Those two . . . they as good as *admitted*

They *did* things
Performed *stuff*
When they . . .
When they did that / *thing* on Grace.

Marianne
Don't get I can't no I don't *go* there that's too

Joff
Did something was something   *summoned* . . .?

Marianne (*puts her fingers in her ears and* . . .)
La la la la la la la

(*Joff watches her until she stops.*)

It *wasn't* fucking . . . *supernatural* shit.
We *agreed*.

All that was fucking *rubbish*.
We *agreed*, Joff.

(*Silence*.)

Joff

So
They were making that stuff *up!*

And that being *so*   *why?*

Joff
I don't know.
I don't know.
I *wish* I could fucking *remember*!!!
Fuck!

Fuck!

Marianne
Calling that crap *religion*!
Saying 'the universe is a construction of divine power'

21

Saying *we* could 'summon up forces'
Saying *everyone* is capable of 'things miraculous'
What did that mumbo-jumbo actually *mean*?
What???

Joff

They said they only ever used it for *good*.

Marianne

'Said,' Joff!
'*Said*'.

Joff

But look what happened!

(*Beat.*)

Marianne

I want *powers*
I want to summon up forces!!!
I want to bring somebody back from the dead!!!
I'll believe in it *then*.
I'll sign in my own blood for *that*!

(*A bolt of incredible lightning.*
And the sounds of strange impossible reversing time
to . . .)

SEVEN

Maud out in the strange terrible weather . . .
It is Then . . .

Maud

Wow! *Wow!!!!*
WOW!!!!!!
Fantastic!
FAN   TAS   TIC!!!!

(And all four are inside, out of the weather . . .
Which circles looking for a way to get to them . . .)

Marianne

Where's Grace?

Ollie

Joyous and she are making up a 'Big Safe Bed'.
And we've got a 'Big Safe Bed' for You Two as well!
But *yours* won't have a 'protection canopy'

Marianne

'Protection canopy'?

Ollie

Two tablecloths and *Maud's* dressing gown!

(Mimes a canopy . . .)

Joff

No protection canopy?
I'm not sure . . .

Marianne

This is *incredibly* kind of you.

(Ollie and Maud demur.)

Maud

Everything okay over there?

(They all go window-wards to look towards Marianne
and Joff's house . . .)

Joff

We've done what we could.

Marianne

Anything *spoilable* is upstairs
Carpets.
Sofa.
Soft Animal Toys Various

Joff

Our daughter is *very* upset we're leaving the majority
of the Soft Toys to fend for themselves . . .

Marianne

But she's got *all* the dinosaurs so –

Maud

How old is Grace?

Marianne

Nine

(*Beat.*)

Joff

Humans all *here*.
That's the main thing.

(*They all look at the house in the weather.*)

Marianne

Now . . .
Fingers crossed

Joff

Everything crossed.

(*Joff and Marianne cross everything . . .*)

Marianne

We're a bit desperate. Sorry.

Ollie

Drinks!
Have some of this white Rioja!

Marianne

Ooh
I thought Rioja was *red*.

Ollie

Not *white* Rioja.

Joff

White Rioja's *white*, Marianne.
She doesn't get out much.

Marianne

She doesn't get out *at all*!
She's a prisoner in a sinking house of Soft Toys !
Not too much.

Joff

A thimbleful. Otherwise . . .

Marianne

Sleep-deprived.
We'll be . . .

(*Both do a very impressive stereo standing dead faint.*)

(*Ollie and Maud look at each other.*
   'Love them for their faults' attitude.
   Until . . . Joff and Marianne recover perfectly . . .)

Sorry!
We get *Silly*
Sleep-deprivation!
Exhaustion!

Maud

That was very funny.

Joff

Sorry.
We're a bit *wired*!
Bit *'men-tal'*
Flooded house! Eek!
Living on coffee! Weeeee!!!!

Ollie

You need a drink a dinner a decent night's sleep . . .
Big plate of our *very own* eggs for breakfast!

Joff

You're allowed to keep hens?
We're not allowed to keep hens!

Ollie

Bantams.

Joff

What?

Ollie

Not 'hens', 'bantams'

Maud

Bantams *are* 'small hens'
Sorry . . .
House flooded . . .
And now you get Ollie lecturing you about poultry
    classifications.
You Poor Things!
Come and Eat!

Marianne

We don't actually *want* to keep hens!

Joff

Bantams, Marianne.

EIGHT

Then.
    All four miraculously sitting at a table.
    *There is possibly food, wine, expensive candles lighting
just the table.*
    Joff reaches for something, puts it in his mouth . . .

Ollie

I assume you've said your own personal thanks for
    the food . . .

Joff
　What?

Ollie
　We always thank God for our food.

Maud
　But if you . . .

Joff
　No!
　Sorry!
　God . . . *sorry* . . .

Marianne
　He's an animal.
　Sorry.

Maud
　Please don't apologise.

　(*She holds out her hands. Ollie does too.
　　No escape. Marianne and Joff take their hands.*)

　Let's thank God together . . .

　(*Ollie and Maud's eyes close.*)

Joff (*silently to Marianne*)
　What the fuck?

Marianne (*silently to Joff*)
　Close your eyes.
　Pretend.

　(*Joff politely closes his eyes . . .
　　Marianne's stay open, on guard . . .*)

Maud (*a prayer somehow*)
　For this strong roof over our heads
　for this shelter from the storm
　for these candles lighting our darkness

Ollie
We give thanks to you

Maud
For the fine food we are about to eat
for this unexpected but welcome company at our table
for our new friends here tonight

All (*with varying degrees of sincerity*)
We give thanks to you

Marianne (*mouthed, to praying Maud*)
No.
Weird!
Don't *pray.*

Maud
For this happy meeting
for your lightning your thunder your life-giving rain . . .

All
We give thanks to you

Marianne (*mouthed*)
Help!!!!

Maud
For this amazing planet we are blessed to live upon

All
We give thanks to you

Maud
For making us human beings your divinely chosen
favourites

All
We give thanks to you

Maud
For exalting us above all animals

All
We give thanks to you

Maud
We love you.

Marianne (*quietest of whimpers*)
NOOOOOOOOOO!!!!!

(*Ollie's eyes open. Fix on Marianne.*)

Ollie (*mouthed*)
We love you.

(*Marianne stares at Ollie.*)

Maud
We think our own thoughts of you in silence.

(*Joff, with eyes still closed, performs a strange
sequence of unlikely contortions.
    Only Marianne sees this.
    Marianne shakes Joff's hand.
    His eyes snap open.
    Odd expression.*)

Marianne (*mouthed*)
Cut that out!

Joff (*mouthed*)
What?

Marianne (*mouthed*)
Fucking *stop*

(*Joff has no idea he has done anything . . .*)

Joff (*mouthed*)
What? *What???*

Maud
For making us exactly who we are

29

For putting us exactly here
Within your shining golden light

All

We give thanks to you

Maud

Amen.

(*Maud's eyes open . . .*)

All

Amen

(*Everybody smiles.*)

Maud

Marianne! Jeff! . . . eat!

Joff

'Joff'

Maud

Joff.

Joff

Please
Dinner!
This is slow-cooked chicken . . . rice 'n' beans . . .
Ollie's special home-made peanut sauce . . .
Jeff . . . if you could help yourself and Marianne to
some of the white Rioja . . .

Marianne

The white rioja is *awesome. Jeff.*

Joff

Joff.

(*And the rain pelts outside . . .*)

NINE

Time has moved on.

Maud

Okay

This is Joyous this morning . . .

'Mummy, why does it rain?'

'Mummy, why does it always come *down* from the
    sky not *up* from the earth?'

Ollie

Stumped!

Maud

'Mummy, it's hailstones when does rain become
    hailstones when it's at the top of the sky or halfway
    down?'

'Mummy, does God make the hailstones or does he get
    his angels to make them?'

(*Maud and Ollie find this adorable, Joff and
Marianne? . . . Nauseating . . .*)

'Mummy, I know what a stone is but what's *Hail????*'

Ollie

The demographic that get asked the most questions?
Mothers

Maud

Two hundred and thirty-eight questions per *hour
    apparently*

Joff

Seriously?

Maud

'Mummy, what is hail *made* of?'

'Mummy, can I go out in it with nothing on?'
'Well then, Mummy, can I go out in it with just
  Daddy's raincoat on then?'

(*Joff and Marianne exchange a look.*)

Marianne

Mothers are actually just the most *ordered-about*
  demographic . . .
'MUM UP NOW! DO THIS GIVE ME THAT NOW
  NOW NOW HERE APPLE CORE! CHOCOLATE
  CHOCOLATE NEW TRAINERS TRAINERS
  NOW!!!'

(*Beat.*)

Joff

Dads only get asked *one* question an hour . . .
Because *we* are the demographic that says . . .

Joff/Marianne

'Ask your mother.'

(*Different qualities of smiles on this.*)

Maud

Ollie's the *big* Answerer around here.
Mr Answers.

Marianne

Joff's Mr *And Swears.*

Joff

Fuck yes

(*Maud winces.*)

Marianne

See what I did there?
Answers And Swears.

Joff

It's not working if you have to explain it, Marianne . . .

Marianne

Joff

a. Don't critique me in public and

b. Don't fucking swear, you're in *company*.

(*To Maud.*) Sorry

He's an animal.

(*A gesture from Maud.*
    Awkward bit of silence.)

Marianne

'Joyous'

What a lovely name.

Maud

Well, so is 'Grace'

Marianne

After Joff's mother.

Joff

And it's a lovely name

Marianne

And it's a lovely name.

(*To Maud.*) Is *your* mother-in-law still alive?

Maud

Yes.

Marianne

My deepest sympathies.

Maud

Actually

I love her very much.

She gave birth to Ollie!

Marianne

Actually

I hate mine very much.
She gave birth to Joff.

(*Joff gives Marianne 'the finger'.*
Marianne blows him a kiss.
Joff mimes dodging it.
Maud and Ollie watch unamused.
An awkward break until . . .)

Joff

Where's 'Joyous' come from?
Is it   a religious thing?

Maud

Just. Came to us.
When she was born.

Ollie

She was just . . . she looked so   full of *joy*
This little baby bundle of *joyousness*

Maud

Her eyes were wide open
And I said 'Hello, You'

Ollie

And she looked back at us
And I said
'Hello
We've been waiting for you.'

Joff/Marianne (*trying*)

Awwwwwww . . .

(*Awkward moment.*)

Marianne

What are those girls doing anyway?
They're very quiet.

(All parents listen.)

Joff
No.
Listen.
Laughing.

Ollie
I think they're watching something.

Joff
I'm watching this rain!
Jesus!

Ollie
Makes you wonder if someone in the neighbourhood
is practising 'pluviculture . . .'

Marianne
Pardon me?

Joff
Pluviculture?

Ollie
Rainmaking.
Making it rain
Conjuring it

Joff
Like a rain dance

Marianne
Like the Red Indians?

Maud
'First Nation', Marianne
Not 'Red Indian'.

Marianne
Okay. Sorry. First Nation.

Maud

Just. What they're called.
Sorry.
Try Ollie's peanut sauce.

Marianne

Okay. Sorry.

Maud

No. Just –

Ollie

Some People believe it's possible to make rain.

Maud

Some People believe its possible to *diet,* darling . . .

Marianne

Some People believe in *Prayer.*

Sorry. Not *your* . . .

Joff

People believe in *any fucking nonsense* given the right
    circumstances . . .

(*Awkward moment.*)

If *anybody's* doing a rain dance . . .
It'll be the fucking *hippies down the road* in their *yurt*

Marianne

Have you met your other neighbours yet?
(*Attitude.*) 'Hugh and Fio-nah'
Jesus!

Ollie

We give the hippies eggs

Maud

We've been to drinks with Hugh and

Ollie

Fiona.

They're charming.

Maud

Ollie. Wine. Marianne.

Marianne

Sorry.

Some *more* of Ollie's lovely peanut sauce, Joff . . .

Ollie

Darling . . .

There's loads more sauce in the kitchen . . .

Maud

Yes! A whole pan!

I'll get it

Don't move.

Nobody move.

(*As she vanishes . . .*)

Ollie

I have to warn you

I'm very very proud of my peanut sauce

Marianne

Sounds interesting

We've never . . .

Joff

What's in it?

Ollie

Well . . . *peanuts.*

Joff

Ha ha.

I mean. What else?

Ollie
  I can't tell you
  Otherwise . . .
  I'd have to kill you!

  (*All three laugh politely as . . .*)

Marianne (*insincerely*)
  That's fun/ny . . .

Joff
  Right. Got you . . . (*Insincerely.*) Ha ha ha ho ho ho.

  (*Marianne and Joff eat. Ollie drinks.*)

Maud
  Ollie!

Ollie
  What?

Maud
  I can't find it!
  I can't find it!

Ollie
  She can't find it.

Marianne
  What's 'it'?

Ollie
  I won't know until I find it for her!
  Coming!

  (*Exits to . . .*)

TEN

Two couples, two spaces . . .
  Dinner table.

Marianne (*a whisper*)
  No more fucking swearing, You!

Joff (*returned whisper*)
  No more fucking *goading*, You!

Marianne
  This is fucking hell on earth this is!

Joff
  And the rest!
  But, we're *stuffed*.

Marianne
  Can't we say we've just remembered some friends we
    can go to!

Joff
  Obvious

Marianne
  Or   your fucking mother's just taken *another* turn for
    the worse
  She's called *in great distress* said
  'I've just plummeted down these perilous steep stairs.
    I'm lying with two broken legs and blood staining
    my beige trouser suit.'

Joff
  Like they'll believe *that*!
  We can't.
  It'd be *rude*.

Marianne
  Do we *care*?

Joff

We have to.
They're our *neighbours.*

One night.

Marianne

Fuck!

Joff

Peanut fucking sauce . . .

(*Both laugh.*)

Seriously
We *have* to stop with the swearing
Every time we swear they're like . . . (*Mimes.*)

Marianne

'Oooh! Language!'

Fuck that!

(*Both laugh.*)

Sshhhh!

(*Kitchen.*
  Ollie and Maud whispering . . .)

Maud

We say your father's just called, he's coming over with
the *entire* church choir they will be singing *very
loud* hymns *all night*????

Ollie

We say we've just been *called*

Maud

Summoned . . .

Ollie

Summoned, very good
To be *chosen* missionaries to spread the word in . . .

Maud

The Congo

Ollie

Deepest

Maud

Darkest

Both

Congo

Ollie

And . . . it is *imperative* . . .

Maud

Very good
Imperative!!!

Ollie

We have to leave *tonight*!!!
An *emergency* mission summons!

Maud

They're *horrible*.

(*Dinner table*.)

Marianne

Do you think Grace is behaving?

Joff

No, of course not.

Marianne

She's in there with 'Joyous' (*As in 'a ridiculous name'*.)
'Our Gorgeous Perfect Girl'

Joff

Perhaps some 'gorgeous' will rub off on Grace . . .

Marianne

A little blob of 'perfect'

Blib!

Joff

Grace is gonna need a bigger blob than *that* . . .

Marianne

You're right.

BLIB!!!

(*Just to be safe . . .*)

BLIB!!!

(*They both look nervously in the direction of the bedroom above . . .*)

Marianne

Silence.
Should we check on her . . .??

Joff

She's quiet.
Found a *friend*.
Result.

(*As . . .
    Kitchen.
    Maud shivers violently . . .*)

Maud

They're so *negative*

Ollie

Coping mechanism
That *impossible* child!
They're just   *unhappy*.

Maud

Do we care?

Ollie

Yes.
I'm afraid we *do*.

Maud
God help us.

(*Dining room.*
Joff gets up.)

Marianne
Where are you going?

Joff
Bathroom.

Pee.

(*Exits as . . .*)

Marianne
But check on Grace.
Make sure she's . . .
And don't get *heavy* with her . . .
Just *talk* to her . . .
You're *always* peeing!
Don't be long.
Don't leave me on my own with –

(*Kitchen.*)

Ollie
One night.
Some kindness.

Maud
Okay.
Anti-Negativity Armour . . . On!

(*They both compete with ludicrous imaginative mimes
for most impressive heavy-duty, complicated anti-
negativity armour.*)

Ollie
Weapons of love and peace . . .

Loaded.

(*And impressive weapons of love and peace . . .*
Kitchen-inspired?
    It makes them laugh . . .)

ELEVEN

Joff, his back to us, peeing . . .

Joff
No
No
Fucking *cross* above the bog?
You're kidding me, right?
Not even *straight*!

(*He adjusts the cross.*
    The tack comes out.
    The cross falls into the pee-filled loo.)

Oh shit.
Shit!

(*He reaches in reluctantly, fishes the cross out.*)

Shit!

(*A sound of wind.*
    A sound of a lock turning.
    A door opens suddenly behind him.
    Turns with wet cross in his hand.
    Covers himself.)

Sorry!
Thought I'd locked it!

(*He turns.*
    No one there.
    He pushes the door closed.

44

Locks it.
Turns to wash his hands.
The cross.
Again.
A sound of wind.
A sound of a lock turning.
Door flings open.)

Hello?

(*Looks for somebody . . .*)

Hello . . .?

Who did that?

Who's doing this?

Grace . . .?
Are you *there*, Grace . . .???
Are you playing silly buggars with me again????
If you *are*, Grace . . .

(*Whatever he thinks he might do, he stops himself.*)

Calm down.

(*Silence.*
He wipes the cross.
Tries to fix it back.)

TWELVE

Then.
Maud and Ollie join Marianne, who is watching the weather over her house . . .
Very small, very covert enjoying of their ludicrous invisible anti-negativity armour and love and peace weapons . . .

Joff joins . . .
All four in the space, but Joff more with Maud,
Marianne more with Ollie.)

Joff and Maud watch as . . .

Marianne, with glass of wine, Ollie with a bottle which
he uses to fill and refill her glass . . .
He is a big practised drinker . . . she not . . .
They stare through the rain towards . . .

Marianne
Water level's –

Ollie
– rising. Oh yes.

Marianne
It'll be up to our bedroom now . . .

Ollie
Yes.
Sorry.
Soft Toys.   Sayonara!

Marianne
Is this what we call an 'Act of god'?

Ollie
Well, I call everything an Act of God

Marianne
No . . . Sorry . . . I mean when we talk to our
    insurance company...
Will this be an Act of God with a big bag of
    compensation money?

Ollie
Well, Acts of God by *God* are one thing
Acts of God in your insurance policy . . . quite another

Marianne

Right . . .

Ollie

Simply . . . in contract law . . .

An Act of God is interpreted as an implied defence
    under the rule of impossibility . . .

Insurers tend to *limit* their liability for an 'Act of God'

More?

Marianne

Oh   no

Oh   well just a . . .

Thanks

You need to read the small print *really* carefully . . .

See what it says about lightning hurricanes earthquakes

Plagues of frogs

Marianne

Well   that's

It's cast iron then.

Surely . . .

Unseasonal crazy weather

Unexpected incredible flooding . . .

Ollie

You'd *think*, wouldn't you?

Except

With *Flood Insurance* . . .

You're literally on dodgy ground . . .

They may have put in something about 'obvious risks'

Marianne

'Obvious risks'?

Ollie

In a lot of cases . . . if it gets to court . . .

The plaintiff loses out by way of ignoring the small
print about

Obvious risks . . .
If you live on a flood plain . . .
And your insurance provider thinks floods are an Act
     of God . . .
You may find they say there is an
Insufficient excuse to perform an obligation . . .

Marianne
'Perform an obligation'?

Ollie
Pay Up. You're very pretty, you know.

Marianne (*beat*)
Thank you.

Ollie
Remember the earthquake in Huensan Province??

Marianne
What?

Ollie
China???

Marianne
Ooo now . . .

Ollie
Earthquake. Thousands of people homeless

The plaintiffs expect a Big Government Payout . . .
but
The Government's lawyers proved the water pressure
from the dam merely triggered an existing geological
fault . . .
Act of God
None of the claims was successful.
Not one.

Marianne
Right. But this is . . .

Ollie
Remember the *mud* volcano in Java?

Marianne
I think I saw someth—

Ollie
The prosecution claimed it was
Provoked by intense drilling.
But the judge ruled it an Act of God
No win.
It's almost always no win with Acts of God
And that's coming from a *believer*.

Marianne
Fuck.
It's our *home*.

Ollie
Get a good lawyer.

Marianne
Aren't *you* a good lawyer?

Ollie
I'm a good *everything*.

(*And he kisses her on the mouth suddenly . . .*)

Say 'fuck' again.

Joff
Sorry . . .

Maud
We enjoy an open relationship.

Joff
Open.
Enjoy.
What does that *mean*?

Maud

It means we trust one another to go away, be ourselves
Discover new things   enjoy other people   and come
   back . . .
Refreshed
Full of love.

Joff

Does it work?

Maud

Mostly

Ollie

I want you . . .

(*Marianne goes somewhere, opens a door . . .*
   Shaft of light . . .
   In the shaft of light
   A girl's shadow . . . a terrible sound . . .)

Marianne

Grace, stop that horrible crying!

What is it?

No, I can't come now.

You're supposed to be in bed.

No.
I'm busy talking to Joyous's daddy about something
   important.

Well, if she's being too rough with you
You know how that feels, Grace!

Liar.

No. No chocolate.

Ollie

Be in charge.
You.
Let her know who is in charge.

Marianne

She's in charge.

Ollie

You need to change that.
Take charge.
Do it.

Whatever it takes.

Marianne

I can't do what it takes.

Ollie

Come outside.
I need to lock up the bantams.
Come with me.
I'll get you a coat.

(*As . . .*
Joff is watching Maud roll some sort of cigarette.)

Maud

You've never . . . ?

Joff

Used to. 'Good Old Days'.
Pre-marriage. Pre-Grace.
Getting out of it!
Waking up next day thinking
'Oh my God, *what happened*?'
Promised Marianne.
She's a bit of a Scaredy-Cat round 'substances'

Maud

It's only herbal.

Joff

It *is*.
Only herbal.

(*Maud lights the joint . . .
Inhales . . .*)

Maud

And   of course . . .
Mind-*expanding*

Joff

Ooooo . . . mind-expanding . . .
Miss that!

Maud

Getting out of it

Joff

Getting out of it

Maud

That journey to the most distant horizon . . .

Joff

Ooo . . .
Thinking 'How the fuck did I get to this distant
   horizon?'

Maud

Where your Brain meets *the power* that *turns* the
   Universe
Peace
Happiness

(*She offers him the joint . . .*)

Take a trip down memory lane . . .

(*Moment.*
   Then Joff takes the joint.)

Joff
   As long as Grace doesn't see
   We try set her a good example.

Maud
   Joyous will set Grace a good example.

   Relax.

   Take a little break from being *a parent.*

   (*Joff carries the joint to his lips.*
      Maud watches.)

THIRTEEN

Time shift.
   It is later . . .

Joff (*it's very painful*)
   She   isn't   good.

   I think I'm a bit . . .
   As soon as she . . . (*arrived*)
   I didn't we couldn't   like her

Maud
   That's sad.
   That's really sad.

Joff
   I was . . . actually, we both were   the word is
      (*very quietly*) 'repelled'

Maud
   No.
   . . . *scared.*

53

Joff
> Honestly.
> Repelled.
> We're still . . .
> She frightens us

Maud
> Sad

Joff
> She won't say what she wants us to do
> We have to *guess*

Maud
> But that's . . .

Joff
> I   last week pinched her   her arm
> Just to
> See if I can make her feel *anything*
> She just smiles
> Like she's *won*
> Like it's what she'd been waiting for me to do . . .
>
> I sometime feel like I want to . . .
> (*Shake her? Slap her?*)
>
> Sorry.
> I *am* . . . (*stoned*).

Maud
> Perhaps she's full of badness.
> And it's not her fault.
> Not your fault.
>
> (*Maud exhales.*
>   *Joff watches.*)
>
> Evil's fault.
> Just   *evil*.
> Sometimes things *take over* people.

Perhaps somebody needs to do something *cleanse*
  Rid her of
Whatever is *in* her

(*Joff inhales.*)

Joff
  Is that possible?
  Could someone . . . can *you* do something like that?

Maud
  God can.
  It's not her

Joff
  Isn't it?

Maud
  You need to be in control.
  You need to believe all things are possible.

Joff
  Yes.

  You're right.
  Yes.

  (*A terrible noise in which . . .*
    There is a dreadful mix of wind, weather, distressed
  hens, trampling . . .
    And confusion.)

FOURTEEN

All four together . . .

Marianne
  I'm so sorry. It's just
  She doesn't *understand* animals.

She thinks they're just Soft Toys!
(*To Joff.*) I *said* we should check on her!

Joff
Yes but *did you?????*

Marianne
Shutupshutup!
We can't take her *anywhere*!!!
Where were *you*?

Joff
One evening off! Just *one*!
Sorry . . .
Grace is just desperate for a pet.

Ollie
They're not *pets*.
They're for our *eggs*.

Maud
She just *crushed* the life out of the poor thing

Marianne
She was just trying to *hug* it

Joff
We're really really sorry.
We'll buy you a new hen . . .

Ollie
Bantam.

Joff
Bantam

Ollie
That doesn't matter it doesn't matter . . .

Joff
It does.
Our kid, our Bad.

Please.
We'd feel better.

Marianne
We're used to it.
Apologising.
'*You know what your kid just did????*'
Compensation.
Grace is just incredibly
Enthusiastic with New   Stuff
So we have to 'expect' a lot of fucking accidents.

She's a *walking nightmare!*

A *disaster scene!*

She's an accident-waiting-to-happen!

Did you not notice she had her *dress* on backwards?

Ollie
No.
She had her top off when I found her.
So I –

Joff
She likes her top off.
She's into Red Indians.

First Nation.

Marianne
I've *told* you not to encourage her in that!

Joff
Allow!
Not *encourage*
There's a *distinction.*

Marianne
Whatever!

However.
Half-naked!
Jesus Christ! Joff.

Maud
Why don't we all just   calm down?

Ollie . . . get everyone something to drink . . .

Ollie
Yes. Sorry. Sorry.

Maud
Here's what we'll do
We'll have a nice drink . . .
Then . . .
I'll show you where you'll be sleeping . . .
Then . . .
Perhaps just a little   time out . . .

Then . . .

Perhaps . . .

We'll give Grace a nice warm bath
With some herbs and nice smells
And something *calming* in there too

Some candles around . . .
Ollie will find some lovely special candles . . . /

Ollie
Yes.

Maud
Perhaps have a little pray together?

How does that sound?

Joff
Sounds like a plan

(*And this plan has a sound like . . . ?*)

FIFTEEN

All four . . .
  Contemplate..
  Two bedrooms next to each other . . .
  A wall of unseeing between them . . .

Maud
  So You Two will be in here.
  Will you be warm enough?

Marianne
  Yes.

Maud
  There's extra covers and throws and shit
  Why don't you make up your bed
  Then we'll sort out Grace . . .

Marianne
  You *do* swear.

Maud
  No I –

Marianne
  'Shit'

Maud
  I apologise.

Marianne
  I don't like you.

  Sorry.
  But I don't.

Maud
  It doesn't matter.
  I give you my love unconditionally.
  I love you.

59

Marianne

No, you *don't*.

Maud

God loves you then.

Marianne

No! He/It/Whatever! *Doesn't!*
It's All Crap.
'Shit'.

Maud

Let's see.
Come down when you're ready.
Then we'll do a little bath . . .
Make Grace all clean again

Marianne

She's not *dirty*

Maud

I just meant a *bath* . . .

Marianne

She's just   a *challenge*

(*Maud enfolds Marianne in a hug.
Marianne stands limp.*)

Maud

I know.
I *know.*
God will help.
I promise.

(*Maud kisses her on the cheek.
Lets her go.*)

Marianne

It's All Crap. (*Isn't it?*)

Maud

Trust me.
God will bless you, Marianne.

(*She joins Ollie.*)

Marianne (*alone*)

Well . . . I've tried *every-fucking-thing else*!
This is your Big Chance!
Do Some Good!
I mean it!

(*Marianne joins Joff.*
It's not a big house.
The walls are thin.
We have to whisper . . .)

Joff

Jesus H Christ This Fucking Situation!!!

Marianne

Shhhhh!
They're like . . . an *inch* beyond this wall . . .

Joff

I'm soooo not keen on *him.*

Marianne

You're not keen on *anybody.*
Why are you *swaying*?

Joff

Because I'm at fucking *sea* here!

Marianne

Stop swaying!
Stop it!
I mean it.

(*The sway-stopping is not completely successful . . .*)

Joff
Wanker!
'Bantams',
What were you two talking about earlier?
You and The Wanker?
By the window?

Marianne
We weren't by the window.
When.

Joff
I saw you.
Talking.
What were you talking about?

Marianne (*infinitesimal beat*)
Insurance.

Joff
You looked *close together*
Like he *kissed* you.

Marianne
You're *still* swaying!!!

Joff
Do you like him?

Marianne
God No!
No!
God!
You were wrapped round *her*.
Do you like *her*?
Mother Fucking Theresa!
'First Nation'
What were *you* banging on about to *her*?

Joff
No idea . . .

(*His eyes start to droop, to close . . .*
   As . . .
   Into sleep position . . .

Marianne
I think *She's* full of shit.
So fucking smug.

Joff
Mmm.

Marianne
'My unshakeable belief in God!!'
Well . . . let's just *test* that shall we, Smugfuck?
Road test their fucking God . . .

Joff
N . . .

Marianne (*opens her mind to that miracle*)
Joff
Should we *do* this thing?
It's . . .

(*He is asleep.*)

Oh *yes*, go to sleep!
Wanker
Joff?
Don't . . .

(*Watches him . . .*)

How come you can suddenly fucking *sleep*?

(*Virtually an inch away . . .*
   Ollie and Maud in their bedroom . . .)

Maud

Have you prayed?

Ollie

Yes.

Maud

I don't believe you.

(*Maud straddles Ollie . . .*)

Liar.

(*Pins him down . . . he tries to escape from her grip.
    She is very strong . . .*)

No.

No . . .

No!!!!

Ollie

They're like *a foot away* from us . . .

Maud

And you *like* that, don't you?

Ollie

No.

Maud

Liar.
Did you come on to her?

Ollie

Of course not.

Maud

Liar.
I think you did.
I bet you did
Did you?

64

Ollie
Shut up

Maud
No, You shut up!

(*And she puts her hand in his mouth . . .*)

You shut right up!

(*And they sex-fight, but Marianne hears . . .*)

Marianne
No!
Don't pray!
I'm a bit up to fucking *here* with your praying
Just cut to a *miracle* okay?
Shut up SHUT UP with the praying!
If you're so fucking *holy* . . .
Just make Grace better!
Listen LISTEN!!!
I'm good.
I'm Good / Too!
I deserve Good Stuff happening to Me!

Maud
Did you kiss her?
With these lips.
With these lying lips.
I bet you did.
You always kiss them.
Don't you?
Don't you?

Ollie
No

Maud
No???
Yes!!!

Ollie
Yes.
A bit.

Maud
'A bit'
A bit like this???

(*She kisses him.*)

Or a bit like *this*?

(*And she kisses him again.*)

Ollie
A bit like that
Ooh yes!
I like it when it feels like you forgive me!

Maud
Yet again.
Yet again My Wandering Love.

Ollie
Say 'Love' again

Maud
Love.

(*Marianne staring at ceiling.*
    Joff, drunken, stoned snooze, eyes closed.)

Marianne
Fake!
You're fake.
One hundred per cent fake.
Therefore
There is No 'God' in You.
Therefore
SHUT THE HOLY FUCK UP!!!

(Joff starts his strange alien movements . . .)

What's going on???

Joff . . .
Why was Grace's dress inside out?
Joff, wake up!
Why was Grace's dress inside out?
When he brought her inside again?
Let's go home!
Get Grace!
We're going home!

(But he will not wake up . . .)

(Then . . . another something . . . something joyful?
   A suggestion of candles.
   A smell of something wonderful . . .
   Some music . . .
   All suggesting some sort of religious ceremony . . .)

SIXTEEN

Then . . .
   Everybody joining after an intense experience . . .
   All somehow changed . . .

Ollie
You see?
God *works.*

Maud
Just left her with Joyous.

Ollie
They're all tucked up.
Under 'the protection canopy'
There's a *lot* of giggling and whispering.

I said 'What's going on?'
They said 'It's secret.'

Maud

They're friends.
Bless Them.

Joff

I expected it to be a bit more . . . (*A mime.*)
A bit more . . . (*Another mime.*)
It was just very *simple.*

Ollie

A nice warm bath
Herbs
Candlelight.
Some prayer.
Not rocket science.

Marianne

She *is* quieter.
She does look

Joff

Happier   seriously

Marianne

Oh please yes

(*It takes a bit but . . .*)

Thank you.

Maud

Not me.
God.
He loves you.

How brilliant is it to have something so powerful
  working for *you*?

(Marianne suddenly hugs Maud tight.
Ollie and Maud look at one another.
Maud hugs Marianne back.)

Ollie
Now   those children go to sleep and
We get shitfaced!

Joff
Sounds like a plan!

(And a sequence of sounds that sounds like a plan.)

SEVENTEEN

It is a few hours and more drinks and smokes later . . .
Marianne, Maud, Joff, all with drinking/smoking
equipage, passing-round, filling-up activity . . .
Eating food randomly and bizarrely, like the very
drunk, very stoned as . . .

Marianne
It's amaaaaazing . . . but I *know*
It's not going to last.

Maud
It *is amaaaaazing . . . and*
It *is* going to last.
She'll be different.
Believe me.

Joff
This is a   tipping *thing . . . point*
Tipping point . . .

(He is tipping quite a bit . . .)

Marianne
Actually . . .

You did very little I mean
You didn't really do *much* at *all* . . .

Maud

I did *nothing*.
Nothing!
He did everything.
Everything.
Have *faith*.
Faith.
Have a *chocolate*.
Chocolate.
Ollie knows this amazing shop . . .

(*And they pick chocolates* . . .)

Joff

You were just *nice* to us.
Nice.
Nice.

Maud

Naaaaa!

Joff

Why can't it be simply . . .
We are born

Marianne

Yes . . .

Joff

We live
We are *nice* to each other
We die
End of story?

Marianne

Yes!
Let's be *nice* to each other.

Like you were to us and our child our Grace tonight.
Very very very nice.

Joff
Good.

Marianne
Yes.

Joff
Kind.

Marianne
Absolutely!

Joff
Why *complicate* it, this notion there's a . . . fucking . . .
    God . . .

Marianne
Ex-actly
Why *complicate* it?

Maud
Because there *is* a God.

(*Stand-off.*)

Marianne
If there's a fucking God . . . *Maud*
Prove it.

Maud
I don't have to prove it.
I just have to believe in Him.

Marianne
Believe *blindly* though

(*Picks up a piece of cake.*)

I believe blindly this cake won't go straight on my
    fucking jodhpur thighs . . .

(*Eats it drunkenly . . .*)

Joff

It's a miracle it's a miracle her thighs remain slender
as a . . . !

Marianne

Twig

Joff

Slender as a *twig*
It's the Miracle of the Thighs and Twigs!

Maud

It's an act of *faith*.

Joff

Leap.
Not just an *act*.
Leap.
It's a *leap* of faith.

(*He does a little leap.*)

You have to *leap* from what is *fact*
To what is *believed* . . .

Like a *chamois* on an *alp*,

(*He does a leap like a chamois on an alp.*)

Marianne

My   *chamois!*

Leap   my chamois!

(*Joff leaps for her delectation.*)

Joff

Leaping is *intuitive*
Not   *intellectual*
Pronking   not   *Proving*

(*He leaps again.*)

Maud

Then okay I had a leap of faith.
I *leaped.*

(*Joff, unseen by Maud, leaps behind her.*)

But when I *leaped* . . . I

(*And again . . .*)

Believed.

I am blessed!
Praise Him!

(*Marianne and Joff stereo cringe.*)

Joff

But. *Facts.* You know . . .?

Marianne

Explain it to us.
Prove it.
Convert us.

Joff

With *Facts.*

Marianne

God knows *We* need something to believe in.
Something *good* something *better* heading our way
Some *proof*
Maud.

Maud

That's not how it . . . (*works*)

Marianne

So *how* does it work?

Joff

Give us the bare *facts.*
I need to pee.

Marianne
Joff!!!!

(*But he's gone to pee.*)

Maud
Marianne.

Marianne
Joff can pee for *England.*

Maud
Take your spectacles off

Marianne (*touching her eyes anyway*)
I'm not wearing my . . .

Maud (*touching Marianne about her eyes*)
You sort of are

Take them off for a second . . .

I don't like *explaining* . . .

(*And suddenly, wonderfully . . . Maud takes Marianne.*)

Come on!

(*And a leap of faith into all the extraordinary weather.*)

Use your *eyes*

Look
Look!
Look!

Marianne
It's all round me and in me!

Maud
Yes!!!!

Marianne
Fucking *Heaven*!!!!

Maud
   Yes!!!

   (*It is wonderful*
     They are flying or something . . .
     Something beautiful and convincing and wonderful
   happens.)

   (*And then, they are back in the drunken room . . .*
     Profound moment of silence.)

   The surprise isn't how you can *believe*
   It's how can you possibly *not* believe???

   (*Joff returns.*)

Joff
   What happened?
   What did I miss?

   Some *leaping?*

Marianne
   Shut up SHUT UP

Maud
   Yes.
   Some leaping.

Joff (*to Marianne*)
   You've lost me

   (*Ollie arrives.*)

Ollie
   I can't find Joyous!
   I can't find Joyous!

Maud
   She's in bed!

Ollie

She's not!
She's not!

Maud

She must have gone to the bathroom . . .

Ollie

She's not in the bloody bathroom!

Joff

I was just in the bathroom

Marianne

Where's Grace?
Is Grace in bed?

Where's Grace?

Where's Grace???

Maud

Joyous!??
Joyous???

(*And they run to find Grace . . .
And then . . . the twelve seconds of terrible chaos.*)

EIGHTEEN

*The terrible thing has happened.
The weather has calmed.
It is cold and still.
Some separate hells . . .
It is terrible . . .*

Marianne

I called her a liar!

Joff

There's all these *bits of time* I just can't . . .

Marianne

I said, 'No, I can't come now.'
I sent her back to –

Joff

Where'*was* I???

Remember . . . *Remember!!!*

Marianne

She said 'I don't want to play with Joyous, she's too
    rough.'

Joff

I fucking   *relaxed*

Marianne

I said,   'Well, you know how that feels, Grace.'

(*Silence.*)

Joff

Did that mean I . . . could have *hurt* her . . .?

Marianne

I didn't believe her
I didn't believe her

Joff

Grace
Was I *there*?

(*They can't breathe.*)

Ollie

I said, 'Joyous . . . can you tell me what happened?'
She said
She said
'We could just *see*'

She said, 'The sky had a lot of   *claws*
And it was trying to open the window
And take the lid off our house and *Grace's* house
And all the bushes and trees were all *dancing*
And the rain and thunder was *drums*
And The Thing said
Come On You Two
I've something to show you.
It'll be Magic!'
I said 'What *Thing, darling*'?

She said 'The Magic Thing. You know, Daddy.'

Maud

Please God
Please
Please
God
Please
Please /
Help me
God
Help me
Help me
Please
God

(*She can't breathe.*)

Ollie

She said, 'We could just *see*.
We went to look at the horse
Then
It galloped away   and
We were all animals all at once!
And
The field stopped being field
And it was *water*

And The *Thing* said
"Dead's *exactly* the same as alive
Come and have a nice bath"
And pushed Grace into the deep water.'

She was copying us, Maud.

(*He can't breathe.*)

Maud
What do we believe in now?
What *can* we believe in now?
What?
Us Ollie
What?

Ollie
Things getting   *better . . .*
Soon . . .

 Eventually . . .

Maud
Name it, go on name *one* certainty, Ollie
One *sure* thing just
One thing *at all* that
You know for certain . . . *is.*

(*But Ollie cannot.*)

One thing.

(*Silence.*)

One thing you believe
You truly eternally *believe*

(*Silence.*)

Yeah . . .
Thought so.

NINETEEN

And they both look towards Marianne's and Joff's house.
  It is now.

Joff
  Look!

Marianne
  Unbelievable!

  (*Marianne and Joff there.*
    It is Now.)

Joff
  Our *Good* Neighbours!
  Was there something?
  Something *we* can do for *you*???

  (*Silence until . . .*)

Maud
  Yes.
  Take us back in time.

Ollie
  Maud . . .

Maud
  And
  When Ollie comes round to your house
  Says
  'Come to us for the night
  You your wife your girl Grace is it?'

  (*Maud looks at Marianne*
    But continues . . .)

  'Have dinner with us I'm making chicken and my
    famous peanut sauce do you eat chicken?'

Say
'No, we're okay, thanks.'
And
Stay   in your own house   and   and
Drown.

(*Silence until . . .*)

Joff

She *killed* my daughter!
Your fucking child!
Who's still *here*!
Who's still fucking *here*!

Ollie

Still *here*???
In what sense is she still *here*???

Maud

You call where Joyous is *here*???

Marianne

Then if she isn't . . .
Look!
It's all up there!
Everything!
Fix it!
Fucking *pray*!

(*And all four are there.
    Around them the weather.
    Above them heaven.*)

Lights down.

End of play.